Super Easy Veget[...]
Cookb[...]

The proven way to los[...] [...]ealth-ily with the ketogenic [d]iet, even if you're a clueless beginner

Table of Contents

Ingredients

Directions

Cauliflower Steak Take

Ingredients

Directions

Limey Creamy Coleslaw

Ingredients

Directions

Cauliflower Hummus

Ingredients

Directions

The Greek Wrapper

Ingredients for the Wrap

Ingredients for the Tzatziki Sauce

Directions

Egg Drop and Zucchini Soup

Ingredients

Directions

Veggie Red Curry

Ingredients

Directions

Chapter 5: Delectable Dinner Goodness

Baked Mushrooms, Italian Style

Ingredients

Directions

Spinach Ricotta Bake

Ingredients

Directions

White Egg Pizza

Ingredients

Directions

Roasted Mushrooms with Feta, Herbs, and Red Pepper

Introduction

You now have in your hands a compendium of knowledge on getting started with a ketogenic or ketosis (keto) diet.

With this book, you have taken the first step towards creating a healthier and more active version of you, and it all starts with a low-fat, low-carb, high-protein keto diet. But first, a little bit about food. Yes, this part is important so hang tight.

Food is a source of fuel. Our body depends on food (and water) to get all the nutrients and nourishment we need to keep us functioning normally. Just like fuel, we should ensure that we are using the good stuff to make the engines of our body run smoothly.

At the same time, food can be something more than merely a source of nutrients. There is so much joy in having a delicious meal that oozes with flavor and character. You get a sense of joy when you dig into a delicious dessert or a lip-smacking starter. It is no wonder that many people around the world explore this planet solely to taste the different foods they can find. These so called "foodie-travelers" live to find out what flavors can be found in countries and locales around the world. They give us a glimpse of all the delicious dishes that they indulge in.

Which is why, when we think of worldly foods, we often think of exotic herbs, meat (all kinds of meat), and spices.

We never think about matching keto with anything exotic or flavorful. Keto is the bland stuff. Keto is for people who don't enjoy food.

A lot of people believe that a keto diet is boring, that there are no flavors to experiment with, and is typically boiled vegetables tossed around with a small helping of salt.

Well, they are wrong. The whole idea behind keto is not to sacrifice flavor. In fact, what you are doing is simply removing ingredients that are not good for you and adding more of the healthy stuff. That does not automatically imply that the food is drab and uninteresting. The reality is quite far from this assumption people make about keto.

So, we are going to take a journey. We are going to be the keto foodie-travelers, and our quest is to enjoy the entire process of keto with some delicious, healthy, and joyful food.

Welcome to the Super Easy Vegetarian Keto Cookbook. Let's begin.

Chapter 1: Keto is the New Hero

The keto diet has been in existence for a long time. Only recently has it been gaining in popularity, though. One of the main reasons is the fact that it is not just something health specialists and nutritionists recommend, but a diet that even doctors themselves have adopted. Don't believe me? Why not check out the YouTube page Doctor Mike, managed by Dr. Mikhail "Mike" Varshavski who has more than 4 million followers as of the writing of this book.

He has been talking about the keto diet for years and even tried it himself!

Before you think to yourself, "Boy, what scam are they selling me this time?" let me assure you that this is not a con or a scam. The keto diet works, and it has shown some incredible results to people who have adopted it.

But then, we haven't answered the important question yet.

What is a Keto Diet?

You see, the fundamental idea behind the diet is to activate your body's own fat-burning mechanisms. This is done as a source of fuel that the body might use for energy throughout the day. This means that the fat you consume, as well as the fat stored in your body, are all sources of fuel that your body can tap into!

The entire process of the keto diet is related to ketosis. That sounds like another fancy term, so what is it?

Essentially, ketosis is a state of the body. It is when the body produces molecules called ketones that are created by the liver. Ketones are created by the body to act as a source of energy to the cells and organs and can replace glucose as a source of fuel.

Our traditional diet consists of carbohydrates and, of course, sugar. Both of these substances produce the glucose required by the body.

However, our body begins to depend on them a lot. Think of it like the body becoming addicted.

How can that happen?

When the body needs to use glucose, it requires the help of insulin, which is a type of hormone in our body. This hormone acts like a messenger and sends information to the cells to open up and allow the glucose to flow into them. The cells in turn send the glucose to the mitochondria, which are the energy generators in our cells.

The more sugar and carbs we consume, the more glucose we have in our cells. Doesn't that mean our body has more energy? Doesn't that imply we could run for 2 miles without breaking a sweat?

The body is a bit more complicated than that.

When the amount of sugar content in your blood increases, so does the insulin levels (to ensure that all the sugar content in your blood gets consumed). When the metabolic functions in the body are normal, then the cells easily accept the insulin produced by the body (these hormones are produced in the pancreas).

However, the metabolic functions do not always remain normal. You see, over time, the cells become resistant to the insulin because of just how much there is in the blood and how often it is produced. The pancreas then goes into panic mode. They need to make sure that the sugar in your blood is consumed. But what can it do?

It produces even more insulin to normalize the blood-sugar levels.

Let's try and see if we can understand the above using an analogy.

Say that you own a restaurant. All the patrons who visit your restaurant are cells, and the favorite dish on the menu is glucose. Lucky you! You have a lot of the stuff. However, you need something to serve all the glucose to your customers. Thankfully, you have your trusty staff of insulin to do the job. Eventually, you realize that you are getting too many orders for glucose, and you are unable to serve the customers. So you decide to bring in more insulin to work for you from the head office, also called the pancreas. Eventually, you realize that you have used all your insulin staff. Your pancreas have no more people to spare for your restaurant. So what do you do? You outsource the insulin from elsewhere.

This is essentially what happens in your body as well. Your pancreas eventually runs out of insulin, which can cause type 2 diabetes. Remember the part about outsourcing insulin for your restaurant? Well, that happens to your body. The only difference is that you are outsourcing insulin into your body in the form of insulin shots or medications.

Let me make something clear – insulin and glucose are not our body's enemies. In fact, do you know the major source of energy for your brain? Why, it's glucose of course! Simply put, you should not cut off glucose from your body.

The problem lies with our consumption of glucose. In today's world, we are spoilt for choice when it comes to fat-induced, sugar-heavy, and carbohydrate-rich food. The idea that more is better is prevalent in our society. Many food outlets and restaurants are focused on adding as much as possible in their dishes, from extra cheesy fries with extra Doritos to that ice-cream churros cookie dessert with chocolate sauce and two layers of extra-sweet waffles.

Wherever you turn, you can find fat, sugar, and carbs waiting for you. While their offers are always tempting, we are going to resist their influence.

Why Choose a Keto Diet?

There are many reasons why one chooses a keto diet. To many, it is the change in lifestyle. They want to switch from a diet that does not give them the right fuel. To others, they want a diet that compliments their workout or exercise routines. While many others want a diet to help them lose weight.

All these goals can be achieved through a keto diet.

Let's take a step back through history. During the time of our ancestors, when they were hunter-gatherers, agriculture wasn't that popular, and the food you consumed depended on what you gathered or killed.

This led to a particular scenario where there might be no food for days at a time. The body had to find ways to keep its human host alive. So when glucose would enter our bodies, insulin would be dispatched to carry it into our organs as well as hoard the unused glucose into fat cells for future use.

This helped our ancestors automatically enter into a state of ketosis; though, our ancestors never knew that. Their bodies would use the stored fats as energy. The result, our ancestors had leaner and healthier bodies since we evolved to consume these fats properly into the body.

Fast forward to the present times. There is no shortage of restaurants, street stalls, and fast-food chains to tempt you into getting something. In fact, convenience is part of lives to such an extent that we can get most of what we want through the touch of a few buttons.

Rather than give our body necessary fats, we are pumping it with more carbs.

Wait, did you just read the fact that we have to give our body more fats? Isn't the point of keto reducing weight?

Before you start wondering whether keto is truly effective or not, let me explain.

There are so many misconceptions about fats. With the way that people around the world treat the concept of fats, it is as though any fat is harmful to our body.

The reality is that we need a certain amount of fats. In fact, we need the good fats. One good group of fats are monounsaturated fats. You can find these in your body in a liquid state when your body is at room temperature. However, they can become more solid when you are in colder or cooler temperatures. These days, you are not going to find any medical professional who has anything negative to say about monounsaturated fats. In fact, they are actually considered good for the heart.

Now, where do we get this good fat?

We can eat foods like avocados, olive oil, many types of nuts, and a host of other ingredients that we will use in the dishes we prepare.

But good fat is not the only thing that we will be consuming. In addition to fats, we are going to make sure we receive the right amount of proteins as well.

All the Wonderful Benefits of Keto Diet

Apart from preventing type 2 diabetes, there are more benefits to keto than you might have originally thought. Let's look at some of them.

Aids in weight loss

Need to lose weight effectively? No problem! With the combination of a keto diet and regular workout routine, you will be shedding weight much better than most techniques. Additionally, once you get used to the diet, you don't feel hungry easily, and the protein-rich food you have aids you in your exercises.

Reduces the risk of diabetes

We saw how diabetes is caused in our body. With a proper keto diet, you are reducing the risk of the disease from occurring. You are giving your body essential nutrients and reducing the amount of glucose you ingest.

Improves heart health

When you are on a keto diet, you are also reducing the intake of harmful cholesterol. This eventually improves the functioning of your heart. In fact, your body's good cholesterol, HDL, increases while the levels of bad cholesterol, known as LDL, decreases.

Improves brain functioning

Many studies have been conducted on ketosis. One such study claims that keto improves brain function (Hernandez et al., 2018). More specifically, it improves cognitive functioning and alertness.

Reduces fat molecules

There are certain fat molecules that circulate in your bloodstream known as triglycerides. These molecules are well known for being a risk factor for heart diseases.

One of the main causes for the increase in triglycerides is the consumption of carbs. This is why, when people reduce their intake of carbs and switch to healthier foods, they begin to notice a decrease in the circulation of triglycerides.

The Bottom Line

A keto diet is more than just a fad. It is a lifestyle sprinkled with benefits. We are going to take full advantage of that. Still with me here? Then, let's head out to our next destination – all the food you can eat and the ones you should generally avoid.

Chapter 2: What to Eat and What Not to Eat

This is an important question and many times, we might often find ourselves feeling lost with different opinions on what exactly should constitute a keto diet.

Thankfully, you have this book.

I am going to list the foods that you can include as part of your keto diet and those foods that you should definitely avoid. First, we will focus on percentages.

When we break down your typical keto diet into its macronutrients, your intake should look like this:

- 75% fats
- 20% proteins
- 5% carbohydrates

Usually, our daily intake of calories should be around 2,000. Which means that if we apply the percentages, fats should provide us with around 1,500 calories, proteins should contribute 400 calories, and carbs should give us the remaining 100 calories.

So, you should be aiming to hit your daily fat requirement, thinking about how much protein you are having, and limiting your carb intake. Then, we will remove any meat products from the list (after all, we are focused on the awesome veggie stuff). Even still, there are numerous foods that you can enjoy on a keto diet.

Since we mentioned the good fats, let's start by looking at the ways you can get some healthy fats in your body.

Healthy fats

Make sure that you avoid trans fats. Bearing that in mind, here are some sources of polyunsaturated and monounsaturated fats:

- Butter

- Coconut oil
- Ghee
- Lard
- Avocado oil
- Extra virgin olive oil
- Macadamia oil
- Coconut butter
- Coconut milk

We are going to have a well-rounded understanding of what foods you can definitely enjoy on a keto diet, the foods that you should keep in moderation, and those foods that are a definite no-no. In short, we are looking at "The Good, The Moderate, and The Bad" foods.

With that established, let's find out about the...

Foods You Can Enjoy on the Keto Diet

When you include vegetables, then you are adding in as many essential nutrients into your diet as possible while reducing calories, which helps you remain within your daily intake goals.

Vegetables

- Artichokes
  - Asparagus
  - Avocado
  - Bell peppers
  - Broccoli
  - Cabbage
  - Cauliflower
  - Celery
  - Cucumber
  - Kohlrabi
  - Lettuce

- Okra or ladies' fingers
- Radishes
- Seaweed
- Spinach
- Tomatoes
- Watercress
- Zucchini

Dairy products

Most people often hesitate when it comes to dairy products because they are often left wondering just what to include and what they should not consume. To put your mind at ease, here are the products that you can definitely include into your diet:

- Brie cheese
- Cottage cheese
- Cheddar cheese
- Cream cheese
- Full-fat yogurt
- Heavy cream
- Kefir
- Mozzarella cheese
- Sour cream
- Swiss cheese

You see? You are still going to enjoy some really mouth-watering food!

Herbs and spices

You have a wide selection of herbs and spices that you can add into your dish. Plus, you are not adding a high amount of carbs or calories into your food, while at the same time, you have incredible flavors to work with. Herbs and spices that you can work with are:

- Basil

- Black pepper
- Cayenne
- Cardamom
- Chili powder
- Cilantro
- Cinnamon
- Cumin
- Curry powder
- Garam masala
- Ginger
- Garlic
- Nutmeg
- Oregano
- Onion powder
- Paprika
- Parsley
- Rosemary
- Sea salt
- Sage
- Thyme
- Turmeric
- White pepper

Beverages

No sweet stuff on the keto diet, of course. That does not mean that you are prohibited from enjoying any flavored beverage. You can still indulge in certain beverages to provide you with a little variety when you feel like having something other than plain water.

- Almond milk unsweetened
- Cashew milk unsweetened
- Club soda
- Coconut milk

- Coffee
- Herbal tea
- Mineral water
- Seltzer water
- Tea

Now that we have a grasp of the good stuff that you can enjoy, let's move on to those foods that you can have in moderation. But what does moderation mean?

In other words, when you are able to get your carbs under control and when you are used to the keto diet, you can make adjustments wherever necessary to enjoy the below foods. This way, you keep your calorie intake within the limit, but at the same time, you can enjoy something you want.

Fruits

There's no doubt about it – fruits are a wonderful source of nutrition. But they also include sugar, and that means we need to be careful about how much and, more importantly, which fruit we consume.

There are some fruits that have low to moderate amount of carbs. You can enjoy these fruits (in limited quantities).

Many of the fruits listed below can be enjoyed on a daily basis, but you might be limited to a cup or a single slice.

Surprised? Did you think I was going to say that you can only have them once a week?

Remember that as you get a better understanding of your calorie and carb intake, you can make adjustments to include more of the fruits below:

- Apricot
- Blackberries
- Blueberries
- Cantaloupe
- Cherries

- Cranberries
- Grapefruit
- Honeydew
- Kiwi
- Lemon
- Lime
- Peaches
- Raspberries
- Strawberries

Nuts and seeds

Nuts are a great source of healthy fats. At the same time, they also contain carbohydrates. Not to worry. They do not have the quantities of carbs that should worry you, and we are going to make sure that you have the right amount.

So what nuts can you have?

- Almonds
- Cashews
- Chia seeds
- Hazelnuts
- Macadamia nuts
- Nut butter
- Pecans
- Pine nuts
- Pistachios
- Psyllium
- Pumpkin seeds
- Sesame seeds
- Sunflower seeds
- Walnuts

With all the keto-approved foods that you can have in moderate amounts listed, we are going to look at all the foods you can't include in your diet.

All the Stuff That's a No-Go

There are numerous categories that you should avoid when you are on a keto diet. You might have heard this one, but it is important to mention it anyways – do not include any food that is a grain or based on grain, as they have a high amount of carbohydrates.

Some of the foods to avoid while on the keto diet are:

- Agave
- All-purpose flour
- Baked goods
- Baking mix
- Bananas
- Barley
- Beer
- Brown sugar
- Buckwheat
- Cake flour
- Candy
- Canola oil
- Cereal
- Corn
- Corn syrup
- Couscous
- Honey
- Hydrogenated oils
- Ice cream
- Juice cocktail
- Low-fat dairy
- Mangos

- Maple syrup
- Margarine
- Milk
- Milk chocolate
- Muesli
- Oats
- Pastry flour
- Pasta
- Pineapple
- Potatoes
- Quinoa
- Rice
- Snack bars
- Soda
- Sweet potatoes
- Sports drinks
- Wheat flour
- White sugar

That's all there is to it. When you look at the list above, you might be thinking if there is any way you can add of one those items as part of the keto diet. Perhaps once in a while won't hurt right?

However, we are going to focus solely on the foods that we can include and not even remotely consider any of the items in the list above. It is not going to be easy, but it is necessary. Once your body begins to understand that it should not depend on carbs or sugars anymore, it is much easier for it to adjust to the keto diet.

Now that we have established the basic guidelines on what you can eat or not eat, let's continue our journey. This time, we are heading straight for our most exciting destination – food!

We begin our adventure in the land of breakfast, the meal that literally means what its name indicates – to break the fast that you have been having overnight since your last meal (dinner if you are following the keto diet, which also means you are bidding farewell to those late night snacks).

Chapter 3: Delicious Breakfast Recipes

Breakfast, the meal that decides just how your day might be. With the right amount of nutrients, you can start your day feeling fresh with bountiful positive energy. If not, you might just feel like you are dragging your body around, with lethargy setting in and your brain thinking about heading back to bed.

Soft Keto Cream Cheese Pancakes

Didn't I tell you this was going to be fun? Yes, indeed. We are starting our day off with soft and cheesy pancakes that will make you want more.

Ingredients

- ½ teaspoon cinnamon
  - ½ packet of Stevia in the Raw (a keto alternative to sugar)
  - 1 tablespoon coconut flour
  - 1 tablespoon coconut oil
  - 3 tablespoons sugar-free maple syrup
  - 2 oz. cream cheese
  - 2 eggs

Directions

1. Take out a bowl and mix all the ingredients together, except the coconut oil, until they are smooth.
2. Next, take out a skillet or a non-stick pan and place it on medium-high heat.
3. Add in the coconut oil.
4. Now add the mixture into the pan and prepare your pancakes normally. The trick is to try and cook as much as possible on one side without burning it. To do this, simply use a spatula to lift up

the side that is cooking to see if it has been cooked thoroughly.

5. When one side is to your liking, you can flip over the pancake and cook the other side.

6. When both sides are cooked, transfer the pancake over to a plate and enjoy!

Keto Spice Latte Boost

Why head over to your local cafe when you can make your very own healthy latte at home? Oh, did I mention it includes pumpkin spice?

Ingredients

- 10 drops liquid stevia
  - 2 tablespoons heavy whipping cream
  - 2 tablespoons butter
  - 2 teaspoons pumpkin pie spice blend
  - 2 cups strong coffee
  - 1 cup coconut milk
  - 1 teaspoon vanilla extract
  - ½ teaspoon cinnamon
  - ¼ cup pumpkin puree

Directions

1. Place a non-stick pan over medium heat.
2. Add in the pumpkin puree, butter, milk, and the spice blend.
3. Allow them to reach boiling point, and once you notice that they are bubbling, add in the 2 cups of coffee into the mixture. Stir the ingredients and mix them all together. Do this for about 2-3 minutes.
4. Once the ingredients are all mixed together, transfer them to a blender, add the stevia and cream. Blend all the ingredients together until they are smooth.

5. Transfer to your favorite coffee mug or coffee flask (that you can take to work).

Smooth Avocado and Kale Smoothie

What do you get when you add in two healthy and delicious ingredients to make a smoothie? Well, you get a deliciously healthy smoothie of course!

Ingredients

- 3 ice cubes
    - 1 cup fresh kale (chopped)
    - 1 tablespoon fresh lemon juice
    - ½ teaspoon liquid stevia extract, to taste
    - ¾ cup unsweetened almond milk
    - ½ cup chopped avocado
    - ¼ cup full-fat yogurt, plain

Directions

1. Combine the almond milk, kale, and avocado into a blender. Run the blender until the ingredients are smooth.
2. Add the remaining ingredients and blend again.
3. Transfer the ingredients into a large glass and drink immediately.

Almond Butter Protein Smoothie

Heading out to the gym? Why not have this drink to give you that boost of energy that you need? Or could even enjoy it on its own while getting ready for your day.

Ingredients

- 1 cup unsweetened almond milk
  - 1 tablespoon almond butter
  - ½ cup full-fat yogurt, plain
  - ¼ cup vanilla egg white protein powder
  - ¼ teaspoon ground cinnamon
  - ¼ liquid stevia

Directions

1. Combine the almond milk and butter in a blender. Let the blender run until you see that the entire mixture is smooth.
2. Add the remaining ingredients and blend again.
3. Transfer the ingredients into a large glass and drink immediately.

Blueberry and Beets Smoothie

What do you get when you add in two healthy and delicious ingredients to make a smoothie? Well, you get a healthy and delicious smoothie of course!

Ingredients

- 1 cup unsweetened coconut milk
  - 1 teaspoon chia seeds
  - 1 small beet (peeled and chopped)
  - ¼ cup heavy cream
  - ¼ cup frozen blueberries
  - ¼ liquid stevia

Directions

1. Combine coconut milk, beets, and blueberries into a blender. Run the blender until the ingredients are smooth.
2. Add the remaining ingredients and blend again.
3. Transfer the ingredients into a large glass and drink immediately.

Almond Muffins with Butter

Crunchy and delicious. The butter adds the right amount of texture to the whole dish. When you want your mornings to start off smoothly, then these muffins can help you with that.

Ingredients

- 4 large eggs
  - 2 teaspoons baking powder
  - 2 cups almond flour
  - 1 cup powdered erythritol
  - ¾ cup almond butter (warmed)
  - ¾ cup unsweetened almond milk
  - ¼ teaspoon salt

Directions

1. Preheat the oven to 350°F.
2. Take out a muffin pan and line it with paper liners.
3. Take a large bowl and add in the flour, erythritol, salt, and baking powder. Using a whisk, mix them properly.
4. Use another bowl and add the eggs, almond butter, and almond milk.
5. Now transfer the ingredients from the second bowl into the first. Mix all the ingredients together.

6. Using a spoon, transfer the batter that you have now into the muffin pan.

7. Transfer the pan into the oven and bake for about 20-25 minutes. To check if the muffins are ready, take a knife and insert it into the center of any muffin. When you remove it, there should not be much of the muffin sticking to it.

8. Allow the muffins to cool at room temperature for about 5 minutes before you serve them.

Classic Omelet, Keto Style!

Sometimes, all you need is a nice omelet to make your day. But you don't want to have just any omelet. What you need is the keto brand of omelets. Like the one below.

Ingredients

- 3 large eggs (whisked)
  - 2 teaspoons coconut oil
  - 1 tablespoon heavy cream
  - ¼ cup diced green pepper
  - ¼ cup diced yellow onion
  - ¼ teaspoon salt
  - ¼ teaspoon pepper

Directions

1. Take out a small bowl and add in eggs, heavy cream, salt, and pepper. Whisk them together until they have mixed properly.

2. Place a skillet over medium heat and add in 1 teaspoon of coconut oil.

3. Add in the peppers and onions into the skillet and sauté for 3-4 minutes.

4. Transfer the mixture in the skillet into a bowl. Reheat the skillet

on medium heat and add the remaining tablespoon of oil.

5. Take the bowl containing the whisked eggs and heavy cream and pour it into the skillet.

6. Cook until you notice the bottom of the eggs starting to set.

7. Here's a trick to getting the eggs right. Tilt the pan slightly to spread the egg and continue to cook until you see that they are almost set.

8. Take the bowl containing the peppers and onions. Using a spoon, spread them over half the egg. Fold it over.

9. Now, just wait for the eggs to cook completely before serving.

Protein Pancakes with a Cinnamon Twist

How about getting the right amount of proteins? How about doing it while having a pancake? How about adding cinnamon to the mix? All good questions that have only one answer, the recipe below.

Ingredients

- 8 large eggs
  - 2 scoops egg white protein powder
  - 1 cup canned coconut milk
  - 1 teaspoon vanilla extract
  - ¼ cup coconut oil
  - ½ teaspoon ground cinnamon
  - ½ teaspoon liquid stevia
  - ¼ teaspoon ground nutmeg

Directions

1. Take out your food processor and add coconut milk, coconut oil, and eggs into it. Blend the ingredients together until they have been mixed well.

2. Add the remaining ingredients into the blender and continue to

blend until you notice the mixture turn smooth.

3. Place a non-stick skillet over medium heat.

4. Add the batter you just prepared in the food processor into the skillet. Do not pour all of it in one go. Use a cup and pour ¼ of the batter for each pancake you would like to make.

5. Cook the batter until you notice bubbles forming on the top of the pancake and then flip it.

6. Cook the pancake until the underside turns brown.

7. Transfer to a plate and move on to the next pancake.

Green Smoothie for Detoxifying

Time to go green in the morning! This smoothie is filled with all the green goodness you can ask for. It's got kale, spinach, and celery. Add a bit of lemon juice and you have that incredible zest to compliment the drink.

Ingredients

- 3 ice cubes
  - 2 tablespoons fresh lemon juice
  - 1 cup fresh chopped kale
  - 1 cup water
  - 1 tablespoon coconut oil
  - 1 tablespoon fresh lime juice
  - ½ cup fresh baby spinach
  - ¼ cup sliced celery
  - ½ teaspoon liquid stevia extract

Directions

1. Combine kale, spinach, and celery into a blender. Run the blender until the ingredients are smooth.

2. Add the remaining ingredients and blend again.

3. Transfer the ingredients into a large glass and drink immediately.

Egg Muffins with Tomato and Mozzarella

Time to try a savoury version of a muffin. The tomato adds in the right amount of sweetness while the mozarella gives the tart flavor to add balance to the entire muffin. Don't take my word for it. Try it out yourself!

Ingredients

- 12 large eggs (whisked)
  - 1 tablespoon butter
  - 1 medium tomato (diced)
  - 1 cup mozzarella cheese (shredded)
  - ½ cup yellow onion (diced)
  - ½ cup canned coconut milk
  - ¼ cup sliced green onion
  - ¼ teaspoon salt
  - ¼ teaspoon pepper

Directions

1. Preheat the oven to about 350°F.
2. Take out a muffin tray and use a cooking spray to lightly grease it.
3. Take out a skillet and place over medium heat. Add the onions and tomatoes. Cook for about 3-4 minutes until the ingredients soften.
4. Transfer the mixture into the muffin cups, making sure that you divide them equally. Whisk them together well. Transfer them equally into the muffin cups. The best way to do this is by using a spoon.
5. Mix all the ingredients together in the muffin cups.

6. Add the cheese on top, pop the tray into the oven, and bake for about 20-25 minutes.

Crispy Chai Waffles

Love the magical flavor of chai? Well, how about transferring those flavors into a waffle. It's east meets west in this easy-to-make and delicious breakfast.

Ingredients

- 4 large eggs (separated into yolks and whites)
  - 3 tablespoons coconut oil (melted)
  - 3 tablespoons powdered erythritol
  - 3 tablespoons unsweetened almond milk
  - 3 tablespoons coconut flour
  - 1 teaspoon baking powder
  - 1 teaspoon vanilla extract
  - ½ teaspoon ground cinnamon
  - ¼ teaspoon ground ginger
  - ¼ teaspoon ground cloves
  - ¼ teaspoon ground cardamom

Directions

1. Take the egg whites and place them in one bowl while the yellows go into another bowl.
2. Start with the egg whites, whipping them until you notice peaks appear on them. Set aside the bowl for now.
3. Move on to the egg yolk. Add the coconut flour, erythritol, baking powder, vanilla, cinnamon, cardamom, and cloves into it and whisk all the ingredients together until they are mixed properly.
4. Add the coconut oil into the bowl with the yolk and continue

whisking. Next, add in the almond milk and keep the whisk going!

5. Time to add in the egg whites. Fold them into the yolk and make sure that the ingredients are mixed in properly.
6. Take out the waffle iron and lightly grease it with cooking spray.
7. For the waffle, pour about ½ cup batter into the iron.
8. Prepare the waffle based on the instructions provided to you by the iron manufacturer.
9. Once the waffle is prepared, transfer it to a plate and work on the remaining batter.

Protein Smoothie with Creamy Chocolate

With the power of the protein and the wonderful texture of the creamy chocolate, you might just make this your preferred protein smoothie. That is, if you are not left wondering which of the other smoothies in this book could be your favorite.

Ingredients

- 1 cup unsweetened almond milk
  - 1 tablespoon unsweetened cocoa powder
  - 1 tablespoon coconut oil
  - ½ cup full-fat yogurt
  - ¼ teaspoon liquid stevia
  - ¼ cup chocolate egg white protein powder

Directions

1. Combine almond milk, yogurt, and protein powder into a blender. Run the blender until the ingredients are smooth.
2. Add the remaining ingredients and blend again.
3. Transfer the ingredients into a large glass and drink immediately.

Vanilla and Chai Smoothie Combo

A bit of the chai goodness with the kick of the vanilla. It's like bringing together peanut butter and jelly, only much healthier and more delightful.

Ingredients

- 1 cup unsweetened almond milk
  - 1 teaspoon vanilla extract
  - ½ cup full-fat yogurt
  - ¼ teaspoon liquid stevia
  - ¼ teaspoon ground cinnamon
  - ¼ teaspoon ground ginger
  - ¼ teaspoon ground cloves
  - ¼ teaspoon ground cardamom

Directions

1. Combine all the ingredients into a blender. Run the blender until the ingredients are smooth.
2. Transfer the ingredients into a large glass and drink immediately.

Protein Pancakes with Chocolate

Consuming protein does not have to be boring. Now, you get your protein in a pancake with some chocolate.

Ingredients

- 8 large eggs
  - 2 scoops egg white protein powder
  - 1 teaspoon vanilla extract
  - 1 cup canned coconut milk

- ¼ cup coconut oil
- ¼ cup unsweetened cocoa powder
- ¼ teaspoon liquid stevia extract

Directions

1. Take out the food processor and add the coconut milk, coconut oil, and eggs into it.
2. Blend in the ingredients using a few pulses. Add in the remaining ingredients.
3. Continue blending until all the ingredients have turned smooth.
4. Add in the stevia for flavor.
5. Now place a skillet over medium heat.
6. Time to work on the batter. Use ¼ cup of batter for each package that you make.
7. Begin cooking the pancake until you see bubbles form on top. Once you spot the bubbles, flip over the pancake and continue cooking until a brown layer forms at the bottom.
8. Transfer to a plate and then use the remaining batter if you like.

Scrambled Eggs with Spinach and Parmesan

These eggs need just the right garnishments to turn them into something special. The spinach does not add in heavy flavors, but the nutty taste of parmesan is a wonderful compliment to both the eggs and spinach.

Ingredients

- 2 cups fresh baby spinach
  - 2 tablespoons grated parmesan cheese
  - 2 large eggs (whisked)
  - 1 tablespoon heavy cream
  - ¼ teaspoon salt

- ¼ teaspoon pepper
- 1 teaspoon coconut oil

Directions

1. Take a bowl and add in the whisked eggs. Add the heavy cream, salt, and pepper in it and whisk again until all ingredients are combined.
2. Place a skillet over medium heat and pour the coconut oil into it.
3. Put the spinach into the skillet and cook until it wilts. This usually takes about 2 minutes.
4. Pour the ingredients from the bowl into the skillet and cook until you see the eggs set. This takes another 1-2 minutes.
5. Add the parmesan.
6. Serve hot.

Cinnamon Waffles

Another waffle option for you. This time, we are bringing in the spicy power of cinnamon with the right amount to vanilla extract to compliment the spice.

Ingredients

- 4 large eggs (separated into yolks and whites)
  - 3 tablespoons coconut flour
  - 3 tablespoons powdered erythritol
  - 1 teaspoon baking powder
  - 1 teaspoon vanilla extract
  - ½ cup heavy cream
  - ½ teaspoon ground cinnamon
  - ¼ teaspoon ground nutmeg

Directions

1. Take the egg whites and place them in one bowl while the yellows go into another bowl.
2. Start with the egg whites, whipping them until you notice peaks appear on them. Set aside the bowl for now.
3. Move on to the egg yolk. Add in the coconut flour, erythritol, baking powder, vanilla, cinnamon, and nutmeg and whisk them all until they have blended together well. Add in the heavy cream and whisk again until the mixture has combined.
4. Finally, transfer the egg whites into the bowl and continue mixing everything.
5. Use your cooking spray to coat the waffle iron and preheat it.
6. Use ½ cup of batter for each waffle you would like to make.
7. Prepare the waffle based on the instructions of the waffle iron.
8. Once the waffle is ready, transfer it to a plate. Use the remaining batter if you like.

Pumpin' Pumpkin Spice Waffles

It's not just the pumpkin puree that brings out the flavor in this dish, but the combination of cloves, nutmeg, and cinnamon. This waffle is a spice fest, and you are invited to try it out (and get hooked on to the dish).

Ingredients

- 4 large eggs (separated into yolks and whites)
  - 3 tablespoons powdered erythritol
  - 3 tablespoons coconut flour
  - 1 teaspoon vanilla extract
  - 1 teaspoon baking powder
  - ½ cup pumpkin puree
  - ½ teaspoon ground cinnamon

- ¼ teaspoon ground nutmeg
- ¼ teaspoon ground cloves

Directions

1. Take the egg whites and place them in one bowl while the yellows go into another bowl.
2. Start with the egg whites, whipping them until you notice peaks appear on them. Set aside the bowl for now.
3. Move on to the egg yolk. Add in the coconut flour, erythritol, baking powder, vanilla, cinnamon, nutmeg, and cloves and whisk all the ingredients well.
4. Add in the pumpkin puree and continue whisking. Transfer the egg whites into the yolk and whisk a little more.
5. Use your cooking spray to coat the waffle iron and preheat it.
6. Use ½ cup of batter for each waffle you would like to make.
7. Prepare the waffle based on the instructions of the iron.
8. Once the waffle is ready, transfer it to a plate. Use the remaining batter if you like.

Keto Tea

A nice cup of tea in the morning? Perhaps to go along with your waffle or pancake? Of course. We even have a keto version.

Ingredients

- 2 cups water
  - 2 tea bags
  - 1 tablespoon ghee
  - 1 tablespoon coconut oil
  - ½ teaspoon vanilla extract
  - ¼ teaspoon liquid stevia extract

Directions

1. Prepare your tea using the tea bags and then set it aside.
2. Take a different container and melt the ghee.
3. Add coconut oil and vanilla to the melted ghee.
4. Pour tea from mug into a blender. Add in the remaining ingredients.
5. Blend them until smooth.

Keto Oatmeal Cinnamon Spice

Sometimes, you just need a good ol' oatmeal to start your day. But no way are you going to resort to the same old stuff. It is time to spice it up a bit!

Ingredients

- 10 drops liquid stevia
  - 3 tablespoons Erythritol (powdered)
  - 3 tablespoons butter
  - 3 cups coconut milk
  - 2 cups cream cheese
  - 1 teaspoon cinnamon
  - 1 teaspoon unsweetened maple syrup
  - 1 cup crushed pecans
  - ½ teaspoon vanilla
  - ½ cup cauliflower florets
  - ¼ cup flax seed
  - ¼ teaspoon allspice
  - ¼ teaspoon nutmeg
  - ¼ cup heavy cream
  - ¼ cup chia seed

Directions

1. Add the cauliflower florets into the food processor and blend them well.
2. Take a pan and place it over medium heat. Add in the coconut milk.
3. In another pan, add in the crushed pecans and cook over low heat to toast.
4. Add the cauliflower to coconut milk and heat the mixture until it starts to boil. When you see it boiling, bring down the heat to simmer.
5. Add in all the spices into the coconut milk and mix the ingredients together.
6. Add the Erythritol, stevia, flax, and chia seeds into the coconut milk and mix them all together.
7. Combine cream, butter, and cream cheese to the pan and mix again.
8. Transfer to a bowl.

Keto Mexican Breakfast Fiesta

Hola and welcome to the dish that will bring in some mexican flavors, all while being keto! Think it impossible? Well, we made possible!

Ingredients

- 4 eggs (poached)
  - 2 tablespoons sour cream
  - 2 tablespoons olives (chopped)
  - 2 tablespoons cilantro (chopped)
  - ¼ cup chunky salsa
  - ¼ cup cheddar cheese (shredded)
  - ¼ cup avocado (chopped into chunks)

Directions

1. Prepare the eggs by poaching them.
2. Next, take a bowl that is microwave safe and add in the salsa. Heat it inside the microwave (which should take around 30-45 seconds).
3. Transfer the poached eggs onto a plate and then top it with salsa, sour cream, olives, cheese, avocado, and parsley.

Shufflin' Breakfast Souffle

This souffle is so soft that you cannot help making a little shuffle after you are done eating it.

Ingredients

- 3 tablespoons unsalted butter
  - ½ cup egg whites
  - ½ cup thinly sliced mushrooms
  - ½ cup fresh goat cheese
  - ½ medium tomato (thinly sliced)
  - ¼ teaspoon salt
  - ¼ teaspoon pepper

Directions

1. Start by preheating the oven to 400°F.
2. Take out a bowl and combine the eggs, salt, and pepper and whip them together.
3. Place a skillet over medium to high heat. Toss in the butter into the pan and wait for it to melt. Add the mushrooms and sauté them until they are soft.
4. The tomato slices go into the pan next. Stir the ingredients a little.

5. Add the cheese into the bowl with the egg whites. Fold them with the whites.
6. Pour the egg white mixture into the skillet.
7. Transfer everything over to the pan and bake for about 8 minutes.
8. Transfer to a plate and enjoy!

Cauliflower Hash Browns

We couldn't complete the breakfast section without having a hash brown recipe thrown in. The best part is that if you need to prepare a quick breakfast, then this is your recipe.

Ingredients

- 2 cups cauliflower florets
  - 1 cup gluten-free flour
  - 1 onion (chopped)
  - 2 tablespoons butter (more if necessary)
  - ¼ teaspoon salt
  - ¼ teaspoon pepper

Directions

1. In a small bowl, add in the flour, cauliflower, onion, salt, and pepper and mix them well.
2. Take out a skillet and place it on medium heat.
3. Add the tablespoons of butter.
4. Take out the cauliflower and flour mixture in a scoop and roll it into a ball. Do not worry if the mixture does not stick together. It will once it has been transferred into the pan. Press on the ball with a spoon until it gains a disk shape.
5. Allow one side to fry and turn a nice brown color. This usually takes about 3-4 minutes. When one side is done, flip it over and

work on the other side.

6. Transfer the hash brown over to a plate. Use the remaining flour mixture for more hash browns. Add more butter if required.

Chapter 4: Scrumptious Lunch Dishes

The afternoons are for taking a break from your heavy schedule or relaxing at home.

The best way to do any of that is by having a healthy and mouth-watering lunch dish right next you, where each bite bursts open with flavors. Welcome to the next step of our journey, where your taste buds will dance, explore, and experience dishes that you might never think could be possible with just vegetarian ingredients.

Well, they are.

Vegetarian Taco Salad with Avocado Lime Dressing

Another Mexican specialty, and we're going to make it keto style. So let's get started!

Ingredients for the Salad

- 15 ounces black beans (drained and rinsed)
  - 4 ounces spring mix (or a mix of your favorite greens)
  - 3 stalks green onion (chopped)
  - 2 roma tomatoes (chopped)
  - 2 tablespoons cilantro (freshly snipped)
  - 2 ears of corn (cooked & corn removed)
  - 1 avocado (chopped)
  - ½ cup cotija cheese (crumbled)
  - ¼ cup tri-color tortilla strips
  - ¼ red onion (chopped)
  - ¼ teaspoon salt
  - ¼ teaspoon pepper

Ingredients for the Avocado Lime Dressing

- 4 tablespoons water
  - 1 avocado
  - 1 tablespoon mayonnaise
  - 1 tablespoon cilantro
  - 1 tablespoon extra virgin olive oil
  - 1 teaspoon lime juice
  - ¼ teaspoon onion powder
  - ¼ teaspoon garlic powder
  - ¼ teaspoon salt
  - ¼ teaspoon pepper
  - ⅛ teaspoon sugar or stevia optional

Directions

1. To make the salad, take out a large bowl.
2. Add all the salad ingredients (keep the salt and pepper for last), and then mix them together. Add in the salt and pepper now.
3. For the dressing, take all the ingredients for the dressing and put them in a blender.
4. Run the blender until all the ingredients are smooth.
5. Next take out a plate and then place the salad on it. Take out the dressing and pour it over the salad.
6. Enjoy!

Egg Salad on Lettuce

A little egg salad makes for a light lunch. But what's the best way to make them? Well, you use the recipe below.

Ingredients

- 4 cups fresh lettuce (chopped)

- 3 tablespoons mayonnaise
- 3 large hard-boiled eggs (cooled)
- 1 tablespoon fresh parsley (chopped)
- 1 teaspoon fresh lemon juice
- 1 small stalk celery (diced)
- ¼ teaspoon salt
- ¼ teaspoon pepper

Directions

1. Take out a small bowl. Peel and dice the eggs into it.
2. Add in the celery, mayonnaise, parsley, lemon juice, salt, and pepper. Mix all the ingredients together.
3. Take out a fresh lettuce and place it on a plate. Add the mixture on top of it.
4. Your egg salad is ready to go.

Egg Soup

Sometimes, you might just want to have a little soup during lunch. Or maybe you would like to use the soup along with another dish. Here's your health egg soup ready to go!

Ingredients

- 6 large eggs (whisked)
  - 5 cups vegetable broth
  - 4 vegetable bouillon cubes
  - 1 tablespoons chili garlic paste
  - ½ green onion (sliced)

Directions

1. Take out a saucepan and place it over medium heat. Add the

vegetable broth to the saucepan.

2. Crush the bouillon cubes and stir it into the broth in a saucepan.

3. Bring it to a boil, then stir in the chili garlic paste.

4. Cook until steaming, then remove from heat.

5. Take out your whisk and start mixing the broth. As you are whisking it, slowly drizzle in the beaten eggs.

6. Allow the eggs to sit for about 2 minutes then serve with sliced green onion.

Spring Salad Topped with Shaved Parmesan

Most of the salads in this book are easy to make, so you can prep them for a quick bite, including this one that combines the kick of a red wine vinegar and the nuttiness of the parmesan to good effect.

Ingredients

- 4 ounces mixed spring greens
  - 2 tablespoons red wine vinegar
  - 1 tablespoon Dijon mustard
  - ½ small red onion (sliced)
  - ¼ teaspoon liquid stevia extract, to taste
  - ¼ cup roasted pine nuts
  - ¼ cup shaved parmesan
  - ¼ teaspoon salt
  - ¼ teaspoon pepper

Directions

1. In a small bowl, combine the red wine vinegar and mustard. Whisk them together so they are mixed properly.

2. Add in the salt and pepper. Whisk the dressing a little and then add in the stevia. Whisk again.

3. In another bowl, add spring greens, red onion, pine nuts, and parmesan. Mix them together.
4. Pour the red wine vinegar dressing on top.

Spinach Cauliflower Soup

How about a little healthy soup to make your day? In this soup, we have the twin benefits of spinach and cauliflower mixed with the creaminess of coconut milk.

Ingredients

- 8 ounces fresh baby spinach (chopped)
  - 3 cups vegetable broth
  - 2 cloves garlic (minced)
  - 2 cups chopped cauliflower
  - 1 tablespoon coconut oil
  - 1 small yellow onion (chopped)
  - ½ cup canned coconut milk
  - ¼ teaspoon salt
  - ¼ teaspoon pepper

Directions

1. Take out a saucepan and place it over medium to high heat. Heat the oil in the saucepan and add the onion and garlic.
2. Sauté for 4-5 minutes until browned, then stir in the cauliflower.
3. Cook for 5 minutes until you see the cauliflower turn brown. Stir in the spinach.
4. Let it cook for 2 minutes until wilted, then stir in the broth and bring it to a boil.
5. Remove the mixture from the heat. Add them all into a blender and then puree the soup. Blend the ingredients until you notice

them getting smooth.

6. Stir in the coconut milk, salt, and pepper. Blend again.
7. Transfer to a bowl and enjoy hot.

Spinach and Avocado Salad with Almonds

Do you have even less time than it takes to prepare a salad? Then, we've got a recipe for you that saves time. If you have the ingredients with you, the salad can be prepared anywhere you like.

Ingredients

- 4 cups fresh baby spinach
  - 2 tablespoons olive oil
  - 1 tablespoons balsamic vinegar
  - 1 medium avocado, sliced thinly
  - ½ tablespoon Dijon mustard
  - ¼ cup sliced almonds (toasted)
  - ¼ teaspoon salt
  - ¼ teaspoon pepper

Directions

1. Take out a bowl and toss in the spinach along with olive oil, balsamic vinegar, Dijon mustard, salt, and pepper. Make sure you mix them well.
2. You are almost done with the salad.
3. You just have to divide them equally between two plates. Top them off with toasted almonds and avocados.

Quick Chopped Salad (When You Cannot Wait)

What if you are truly in a hurry and would like to shorten the prep time for your salad. Well, you can use the below recipe to dig into a delicious salad even faster than the previous recipe.

Ingredients

- 4 cups fresh chopped lettuce
  - 2 hard-boiled eggs (peeled and sliced)
  - 1 small avocado (pitted and chopped)
  - ½ cup cherry tomatoes (halved)
  - ½ cup shredded cheddar cheese
  - ¼ cup diced cucumber

Directions

1. Divide the lettuce between two salad plates or bowls.
2. Top the salads with diced avocado, tomato, and celery.
3. Add the sliced egg and shredded cheese.
4. Serve the salads with your favorite keto-friendly dressing.
5. That's all there is to it! Pretty quick isn't it?

Avocado, Lettuce, and Tomato Sandwich

Sometimes, all you need is a nice sandwich for lunch. The avocado and lettuce add the perfect texture to the sandwich while the sweetness of the tomato makes for a wonderful addition. And guess what? We are going to be making the bread in our trusted ovens!

Ingredients

- 1 large egg (separated)
  - 1 slice tomato
  - 1 ounce cream cheese, softened

- ¼ teaspoon cream of tartar
- ¼ teaspoon salt
- ¼ cup sliced avocado
- ¼ cup shredded lettuce

Directions

1. We will start with the bread first. Preheat the oven to 300°F.
2. Take out a baking tray and line it with parchment paper.
3. In a bowl, beat the egg whites with the cream of tartar and salt until soft peaks form.
4. In a separate bowl, add in cream cheese and egg yolk until smooth and pale yellow. Whisk all the ingredients together.
5. Now take the egg whites and fold them into the second bowl a little at a time until smooth and well combined.
6. Take out the batter using a spoon and spread it around onto the parchment paper into two even circles.
7. Bake for about 25 minutes until you start to notice that the bread has become firm with a light brown color.
8. Take out the bread and finish the preparation by adding in the avocado, lettuce, and tomato.

Artichoke and Spinach Casserole

By adding two different cheese into this dish, you are adding a rich and creamy texture while playing with some incredible flavors. The red pepper is going to add that spicy kick without being too much for your taste buds to handle. After all, we want to tickle your tongue, not burn it!

Ingredients

- 16 large eggs
  - 2 cups artichoke hearts
  - 2 cups spinach (cleaned and drained well)

- 1 cup white cheddar
- 1 teaspoon salt
- 1 clove garlic (minced)
- ½ cup parmesan cheese
- ½ cup ricotta cheese
- ½ teaspoon dried thyme
- ½ teaspoon crushed red pepper
- ¼ cup onion (chopped)
- ¼ cup milk

Directions

1. Preheat the oven to 350°F. Take out a baking dish and spray it with cooking spray. Crack the eggs into a large bowl and add the milk. Whisk the eggs well to combine.
2. Take another bowl and break the artichoke hearts up into small pieces into it. Separate the leaves. Use paper towels to remove any excess liquid from the spinach.
3. Add both the artichokes and the spinach to the egg mixture. Add all remaining ingredients, except the ricotta cheese, and stir to combine.
4. Pour the mixture into the baking dish.
5. Take out the cheese and spread it evenly over the casserole.
6. Pop the baking dish into the oven and bake for about 30-35 minutes.
7. To test if your casserole has been well cooked, take out the dish and shake it a little. If the center of the dish does not jiggle, then you have yourself a well-cooked casserole!

Shaking Shakshuka!

Shakshuka is a hearty meal that can be enjoyed anytime, even during breakfast or dinner. Even the name itself is fun! Imagine telling someone that you are preparing shakshuka. That will definitely raise the curiosity levels of anyone. Do not worry about the pepper that we are going to add. The sweet marinara sauce will prevent it from getting too hot to handle.

Ingredients

- 4 eggs
  - 1 cup marinara sauce
  - 1 chili pepper
  - 1 teaspoon fresh basil
  - ¼ cup feta cheese
  - ¼ teaspoon cumin
  - ¼ teaspoon salt
  - ¼ teaspoon pepper

Directions

1. Start by preheating the oven to about 400°F.
2. Take out a skillet and place it over medium heat. Add the marinara and the pepper into the skillet. Allow the pepper to cook into the marina. This should take about 5 minutes.
3. Crack and gently add your eggs into the marinara sauce.
4. Next, sprinkle feta cheese all over the eggs and season with salt, pepper and cumin. Make sure you spread the cheese evenly over the marinara.
5. Usually, people might ask you to transfer the marinana mixture into a baking tray. But this time, we won't be doing that. We are going to transfer the skillet itself into the oven! Convenient huh?
6. Allow the skillet to remain in the oven for about 10 minutes.
7. Once you notice that the eggs are cooked (but are still runny), take out the skillet from the oven.

8. And that's it! Transfer the dish to a plate and enjoy!

Cheese and Broccoli Fritters

Enjoying fritters does not mean that you have to give up on flavors. It just means that you are going to use some wonderful and healthy ingredients to get incredible results. For this dish, we are going to prepare the dish and a sauce as well!

Ingredients for the Fritters

- 7 tablespoons flaxseed meal
    - 2 large eggs
    - 2 teaspoons baking powder
    - ¾ cup almond flour
    - ½ cup mozzarella cheese
    - ½ cup fresh broccoli
    - ¼ teaspoon salt
    - ¼ teaspoon pepper

Ingredients for the Sauce

- ½ tablespoon lemon juice
    - ¼ cup mayonnaise
    - ¼ cup fresh chopped dill
    - ¼ teaspoon salt
    - ¼ teaspoon pepper

Directions

1. Take out a food processor and add in the broccoli. Blend until you see it getting smooth.
2. Put the blended broccoli into a bowl. Mix together the cheese, almond flour, 4 tablespoons flaxseed meal and baking powder

with the broccoli.

3. Add the 2 eggs and mix all the ingredients together well until everything is mixed well.

4. Roll the batter into balls. Coat with a little flaxseed meal. Continue doing this with the remaining batter. You can use a paper towel to hold all the batter.

5. Time to get out your deep fryer. Preheat it to around 375°F.

6. Take out the basket and place the broccoli and cheese fritters inside it. Make sure that you are not crowding it too much.

7. Fry the fritters until golden brown, about 3-5 minutes.

Stuffed Zucchini with Marinara

Making a stuffed zucchini is not complicated, as you will notice from this dish. The best part is that you can actually prepare them for your friends or family and show off your cooking skills.

Ingredients

- 4 medium-sized zucchini
  - 1-½ cups marinara sauce
  - ½ cup goat cheese
  - 1 teaspoon chopped parsley

Directions

1. Preheat the oven to 400°F.

2. Slice the zucchini in half lengthwise and scoop out the seeds, leaving the zucchini hollowed out.

3. Line up a baking tray with sheet and then place the zucchini on top of it.

4. Season with kosher salt and freshly ground black pepper.

5. Using half of the goat cheese that you have with you, spread a small amount in the bottom of each zucchini.

6. Spoon marinara sauce on top. Sprinkle the remaining goat cheese evenly on top of the sauce.

7. Place the baking tray in the oven then bake the zucchini until goat cheese is soft and marinara is bubbling.

8. This usually takes about 10 minutes.

9. You are ready to eat your zucchini or show off your skills to others.

Cauliflower Steak Take

One of the changes you start noticing on the keto diet is the fact that if you did not like cauliflower before, you just begin to enjoy it now because of the variety of ways in which you can cook them. If you already liked cauliflower before, then this recipe is going to create a newfound love for the vegetable.

Ingredients

- 4 tablespoons butter
  - 2 tablespoons seasoning blend (get your favorite one)
  - 1 large head cauliflower
  - 1 teaspoon salt
  - ¼ cup parmesan cheese
  - ¼ teaspoon pepper

Directions

1. Preheat the oven to 400°F.

2. If the cauliflower that you bought has leaves on it, then remove them.

3. Slice the cauliflower lengthwise, starting from the top and slicing all the way through the core. Using this method, make slices of cauliflowers that are ideally 1 inch thick.

4. Melt butter inside a microwave. Take it out and add the

seasoning to it. Make a paste out of the butter.

5. Using a brush, coat the cauliflowers with the spiced butter.
6. Sprinkle with salt and pepper.
7. Place a nonstick pan over medium heat. Place the cauliflower steaks on the pan and cook them for about 2-3 minutes or until they turn a shade of light brown.
8. Once one side is browned, flip over the steaks and cook the other side.
9. Take out a baking tray and line it with a sheet. Place the cauliflowers on the baking sheet.
10. Pop the tray into the over and bake the cauliflowers for about 15-20 minutes.
11. Take it out of the oven, sprinkle with some parmesan cheese and serve while hot.

Limey Creamy Coleslaw

This coleslaw is the perfect accompaniment to any of the dinner dishes that you have seen here. But if you are in the mood for something light, then you can have this on your own. The trick to this dish is the lime and the kick that it adds to all the flavors.

Ingredients

- 2 limes (juiced)
    - 1-½ cups coleslaw
    - 1-½ avocados
    - 1 garlic clove
    - 1 teaspoon cilantro
    - ½ teaspoon salt
    - ¼ cup cilantro leaves
    - ¼ cup water

Directions

1. In a food processor add the garlic and cilantro and blend them together until chopped.
2. Add the lime juice, avocados, and water. Continue blending until everything is nice and creamy.
3. Take out the avocado mixture, and in a large bowl, mix it with the coleslaw. It will be a bit thick, but it will cover the slaw nicely.
4. For best results, refrigerate for a few hours before eating to soften the cabbage.

Cauliflower Hummus

Think about some of the dinner recipes right here. Wouldn't it be better if there was some kind of dip or sauce to go along with it? Your wish has been answered.

Ingredients

- 3 cups raw cauliflower florets
  - 3 whole garlic cloves
  - 3 tablespoons extra virgin olive oil
  - 3 tablespoons lemon juice
  - 2 tablespoons water
  - 2 raw garlic cloves (crushed – these are additional garlic cloves that will be used separately)
  - 2 tablespoons extra virgin olive oil
  - 1-½ tablespoons tahini paste
  - ¾ teaspoon kosher salt
  - ½ teaspoon smoked paprika

Directions

1. Take out a dish that is microwave safe and then combine the cauliflower, water, 2 tablespoons of olive oil, about ½ teaspoon of kosher salt, and the 3 whole garlic cloves.
2. Place the bowl into a microwave for about 15 minutes or until softened and darkened in color.
3. Put the cauliflower mixture into a blender and let the machine run. Add the tahini paste, lemon juice, 2 raw garlic cloves, 3 tablespoons of olive oil, and the remaining kosher salt. Blend them all together until they look smooth. If you would like to add more flavors, taste the puree and make adjustments.
4. To serve, place the hummus in a bowl and drizzle with extra virgin olive oil and a sprinkle of paprika. Use thinly sliced tart apples, celery sticks, raw radish chips, or other veggies to dip with.

The Greek Wrapper

We are going to take a trip to Greek to wrap ourselves in their cuisine (no pun intended). Let's check out a unique way to have your veggies.

Ingredients for the Wrap

- 8 whole kalamata olives (halved)
  - 4 large cherry tomatoes (halved)
  - 4 large collard green leaves (washed)
  - 1 medium cucumber (sliced)
  - ½ medium red bell pepper (sliced)
  - ½ cup purple onion (diced)
  - ½ block feta (cut into strips)

Ingredients for the Tzatziki Sauce

- 2 tablespoons olive oil
  - 2 tablespoons minced fresh dill
  - 1 cup full-fat plain Greek yogurt
  - 1 teaspoon garlic powder
  - 1 tablespoon white vinegar
  - ¼ cup cucumber (seeded and grated)
  - ¼ teaspoon salt
  - ¼ teaspoon pepper

Directions

1. Take out a bowl and mix all the ingredients for the tzatziki sauce together. Once they are mixed, store in the fridge. Be sure to squeeze all the water out of the cucumber after you grate it.
2. Now we are going to prepare collard green wraps. We start off by washing the leaves well and trimming the fibrous stem from each leaf.
3. Spread 2 tablespoons of tzatziki onto the center of each wrap and spread the sauce around.
4. Add the cucumber, pepper, onion, olives, feta, and tomatoes in the center of the wrap.
5. Fold the wrap like you are folding a burrito. If you haven't folded a burrito before, then don't worry! Here is how you do it. You start off by folding each side toward the center. You then fold the rounded end over the filling and roll.
6. And that's it! You can slice the wrap in halves and serve with any leftover tzatziki or wrap in plastic for a quick lunchtime meal!

Egg Drop and Zucchini Soup

This soup comes with a nice little surprise. It's got noodles! In fact, you might not believe what these noodles are made from. The entire dish is hearty, filling, and just oozing with that nice minced garlic flavor.

Ingredients

- 8 cups vegetable broth (divided)
  - 5 cups shiitake mushrooms (sliced)
  - 5 tablespoons low-sodium soy sauce
  - 4 medium to large zucchinis
  - 4 large eggs (beaten)
  - 3 tablespoons cornstarch
  - 2 tablespoons extra virgin olive oil
  - 2 cups water (divided into 1 cup)
  - 2 tablespoons minced ginger
  - 2 cups thinly sliced scallions (divided)
  - ½ teaspoons red pepper flakes
  - ½ teaspoons salt
  - ½ teaspoons pepper

Directions

1. The first thing that we have to do is create zucchini noodles. We are going to first cut the tops off the zucchini. Then, cut the zucchini into two halves.
2. Next, we are going to run the zucchini through a spiralizer. Once you do that, you have yourself some really cool noodles! Wait, you thought we were going to use store bought noodles? No way!
3. In a large pot, heat the olive oil over medium-high heat.
4. Add the minced ginger and cook, stirring, for 2 minutes.
5. Add the shiitake mushrooms and a tablespoon of water and

cook until the mushrooms begin to sweat.

6. Add 7 cups of the vegetable broth, the remaining water, the red pepper flakes, tamari sauce, and 1-½ cups of chopped scallions. Bring to a boil, stirring occasionally.

7. Meanwhile, mix the remaining cup of vegetable broth with the cornstarch and whisk until completely smooth.

8. While stirring the soup, slowly pour in the beaten eggs in a thin stream. Continue stirring until all of the egg is incorporated.

9. Slowly pour the cornstarch mixture into the soup and cook for about 4-5 minutes to thicken.

10. Season to taste with salt and pepper (usually I add just a bit of pepper, but as long as I'm using a full-sodium vegetable broth, I don't need any extra salt).

11. Add the spiralized zucchini noodles to the pot and cook, stirring, for about 2 minutes, or until the noodles are just soft and flexible (remember, they'll continue cooking in your bowl!).

12. Serve topped with the remaining scallions.

13. Who would have thought noodles could be made from zucchini right?

Veggie Red Curry

Ever heard of Thai red curry? Have you ever tried it? Well, welcome to the world of the veggie red curry. Oh and it will still include the coconut flavor so popular with traditional red curries.

Ingredients

- 4 tablespoons coconut oil
  - 2 teaspoons soy sauce
  - 1 cup broccoli florets
  - 1 teaspoon minced garlic

- 1 tablespoon red curry paste
- 1 teaspoon minced ginger
- 1 large handful of spinach
- ½ cup coconut cream (or coconut milk)
- ¼ medium onion

Directions

1. Place a pan on medium heat and add about 2 tablespoons of the oil into it.
2. When the oil is hot, add the onion to the pan and let it sizzle. Allow it to cook for 3-4 minutes to caramelize and become semi-translucent.
3. Once this happens, add the garlic to the pan and let it brown slightly. This typically takes around 30 seconds.
4. Turn the heat to medium-low and add broccoli florets to the pan. Stir everything together well. Let the broccoli take on the flavors of the onion and garlic. This should take about 1-2 minutes.
5. Move everything in your pan to the side and add 1 tablespoon red curry paste. You want this hitting the bottom of the pan so that all the flavors can be released from the spices.
6. Once your red curry paste starts to smell pungent, mix everything together again and add a large handful of spinach over the top.
7. Allow the spinach to wilt a little. Once it has done that, add the coconut milk into the dish and mix everything well.
8. Stir everything together and then add the remaining 2 tablespoons of coconut oil, 2 tablespoons soy sauce, and minced ginger. Let all the ingredients simmer for 5-10 minutes, depending on how thick you want the sauce.
9. That's it. Take out the dish and serve. You can easily compliment the red curry with the fritters' recipe that was mentioned earlier.

Chapter 5: Delectable Dinner Goodness

Dinnertime is all about sitting down in front of a delicious meal. You can choose to have the meal by itself or while watching your favorite movie.

The important thing is that you are having something that not only fills your stomach until the next day, but does not make you feel bloated (which is not something you want to experience right before you go to bed).

Below, you are going to some carefully selected dinner recipes that can go well on their own or along with your favorite smoothie recipe from Chapter 3.

Onwards to wonderful dinner secrets and tasteful dishes.

Baked Mushrooms, Italian Style

Everyone loves some mushrooms. So let's bring in the flavors of Italy into this dish that really look simple to prepare but has so much going on with it. The end result – something beautiful to look at and delicious to dig into.

Ingredients

- 4 Portobello mushrooms
  - 2 tablespoons ghee
  - 2 tablespoons fresh basil
  - 1 cup grated parmesan cheese
  - 1 large can tomatoes (unsweetened)
  - 1 tablespoon fresh parsley
  - 1 teaspoon dried oregano
  - ¼ teaspoon salt (2 spoons of ¼ each – 1 for the mushrooms and 1 later for the canned tomatoes)
  - ¼ teaspoon pepper

Directions

1. Preheat the oven to 400°F.
2. Next, clean the mushrooms and slice them however you like.
3. Take out a nonstick pan and place it over medium heat. Add in your ghee into the pan.
4. Toss in your mushrooms into the pan and season it with your salt and pepper. Mix everything and allow the ingredients to cook for about 5 minutes.
5. Take out a baking tray and place the mushrooms inside them.
6. Wash the basil, parsley, and organo. Chop them up well.
7. In a bowl, add canned tomatoes and layer it with the herbs you just chopped. Add the remaining salt into the dish.
8. Top it all off with your grated parmesan.
9. Place your baking tray into the oven for about 25 minutes.
10. After that, take it out and place it on a cooling rack or any other surface to cool for about a couple of minutes.

Spinach Ricotta Bake

Why not go crazy for some ricotta? And while you are at it, why not add in two more types of cheese to get the cheesiest party started on your taste buds (no pun intended again)?

Ingredients

- 4 cups frozen spinach
  - 2 eggs
  - 2 cups ricotta
  - 1 garlic clove (finely chopped)
  - 1 tablespoon extra virgin olive oil
  - 1 teaspoon sprinkle of organic broth granules
  - ½ teaspoon alt

- ½ teaspoon nutmeg
- ½ teaspoon paprika
- ½ teaspoon pepper
- ½ cup mozzarella
- ¼ cup double cream
- ¼ cup parmesan

Directions

1. Take out a wok and place it over medium to high heat. Add in the olive oil.
2. Add spinach, garlic, broth granules, pepper, nutmeg, and paprika.
3. Stir and cook until the ingredients look dry. Set aside the wok to cool.
4. Preheat oven to 400°F.
5. Now take the eggs into a bowl and whisk them.
6. Add ricotta and whisk again. Add the cream and continue whisking.
7. Add ¼ salt, the spinach from the wok (which should be cooled by now), half of the parmesan, and all the mozzarella.
8. Stir everything together. Now take out a baking tray and layer the ingredients into it.
9. Use a spoon to make the surface even. Add the remaining parmesan evenly on top.
10. Bake for about 40-50 minutes or until the top layer takes on a brown coating.
11. Once done, take out the dish and serve.

White Egg Pizza

If you are planning a pizza party, forget getting them from the local chain where you are most probably going to be digging into a lot of fat and grease. Try this healthy option instead.

Ingredients

- 2 tablespoons extra virgin olive oil
  - 2 tablespoons egg fast alfredo sauce
  - 2 large eggs
  - 2 tablespoons monterey jack cheese (shredded)
  - 1 tablespoon water
  - 1 tablespoon green onion (chopped)
  - ½ teaspoon cumin
  - ½ teaspoon kosher salt
  - ½ teaspoon pepper
  - ½ pickled jalapeno (minced)

Directions

1. Begin by preheating oven to 350°F.
2. Take out a pan and place it over medium to high heat. Add in the olive oil. Spread the oil around to the sides of the pan as well as best as you can.
3. Add cumin, kosher salt, and pepper to the eggs in a bowl. Add the water and beat until frothy using a fork or a whisk.
4. Pour the eggs the pan and cook them until eggs are set on the bottom.
5. You might notice that the top might look a little wobbly. But that is okay! They will still be a little moist and wobbly on top.
6. Add the egg fast alfredo sauce and half of the chopped pickled jalapeno. Add shredded cheese and green onion. Mix them all well.

7. Now transfer the pan itself into the oven, preferably on the top rack.
8. Bake for about 3-5 minutes.
9. Take it out and enjoy!

Roasted Mushrooms with Feta, Herbs, and Red Pepper

Everyone loves some mushrooms. So let's bring in the flavors of Italy into this dish that really looks simple to prepare but has so much going on with it. The end result; – something beautiful to look at and delicious to dig into.

Ingredients

- 12 ounces of jar-roasted red pepper (drained and chopped into small pieces)
  - 4 tablespoons extra virgin olive oil
  - 3 tablespoons fresh lemon juice
  - 2 tablespoons fresh mint (chopped)
  - 2 tablespoons fresh oregano (chopped)
  - 2 cups fresh brown mushrooms
  - ½ teaspoon salt
  - ½ teaspoon pepper
  - ¼ cup feta cheese

Directions

1. Begin by preheating the oven to 450°F. Take out a roasting pan and line it with aluminum foil.
2. Take a small bowl and mix about 2 tablespoons of the olive oil, lemon juice, red pepper, mint, and oregano. Mix all the ingredients well and then set them aside to marinate.

3. Wash the mushrooms and then cut them into quarters.

4. Cut large mushrooms into quarters. Take another bowl and add in the mushrooms, the remaining 2 tablespoons of oil, salt, and pepper.

5. Arrange the mushrooms on the roasting pan. Pop the pan into the oven.

6. Let the mushrooms roast for about 15 minutes or until mushrooms are starting to get brown.

7. Take out the pan, turn the mushrooms over and then roast them for about 5 minutes more. At this point, the mushrooms should be brown all over. If not, then place them into the oven and roast again for another 3 minutes.

8. Place the mushrooms back into the bowl that you took them out of. Add in the red pepper mixture into the bowl and mix well.

9. Arrange the mushrooms on a plate. Sprinkle the feta cheese on top, and serve.

Eggplant Hash, The Moroccon Way

More hash for you, but this time, we are going to try it out in a Moroccan style. Sounds adventurous? Then let's get started.

Ingredients

- 4 garlic cloves (minced)
  - 2 tablespoons ghee
  - 2 small red bell peppers (seeded and cubed)
  - 1 large eggplant (peeled, cubed and salted)
  - 1 medium red onion (diced)
  - ½ teaspoon ground cinnamon
  - ½ teaspoon coriander seed
  - ½ teaspoon cayenne powder

- ½ teaspoon salt
- ½ teaspoon pepper
- ¼ cup slivered almonds (toasted)
- ½ cup sun-dried tomatoes
- ¼ cup fresh mint leaves

Directions

1. Pre-heat a really large sauté pan or wok over high heat. Add your oil and swirl it around to coat the pan. Quickly add your eggplant and peppers. Add salt and pepper.
2. Toss the veggies in the pan to coat with the oil, then allow them to sit in the pan and sear for about 1 minute. Make sure they are evenly spread on the bottom of the pan and not piled up in one part. Toss them and spread them out to sear for another minute.
3. After about 2 to 3 minutes, add your onions and garlic, then toss the ingredients together and allow them to sit for about 2 more minutes. Season with a little salt and pepper and then toss and spread and then allow the veggies to sear for another minute or two.
4. Add your almonds, sun-dried tomatoes, and fresh mint leaves. Mix the ingredients well. You are only looking to heat up the new ingredients. They don't need any further cooking.
5. Taste your hash. If it needs a little more salt and pepper, add it. Finally, sprinkle the spices on top of all the ingredients, mix everything together.
6. Serve while hot!

Falafel with Tahini Sauce

This Middle Eastern delight is a vegetarian's dream come true. You might also find them added to sandwiches or wraps. But this time, we are going to enjoy them by themselves, with a generous helping of tahini sauce.

Ingredients for the Falafel

- 3 tablespoons coconut flour
  - 2 tablespoons fresh parsley (chopped)
  - 2 large eggs
  - 1 cup raw cauliflower (pureed)
  - 1 teaspoon kosher salt
  - 1 tablespoon ground cumin
  - 1 tablespoon olive oil
  - 1 clove garlic (minced)
  - ½ cup ground slivered almonds
  - ½ tablespoon ground coriander
  - ½ teaspoon cayenne pepper

Ingredients for Tahini sauce

- 3 tablespoons water
  - 2 tablespoons tahini paste
  - 1 tablespoon lemon juice
  - 1 clove garlic (minced)
  - ½ teaspoon salt

Directions

1. Firstly, chop up the cauliflower and then add it to the blender. Run the machine until all the ingredients are blended together and the mixture turns smooth.
2. Add in the almonds as well but make sure that you do not over grind them, you want the crunchy texture to remain.
3. Take out a medium bowl and then combine the ground cauliflower and ground almonds. Add the rest of the

ingredients and mix them really well.

4. Take out a pan and place it on medium heat. Add in the olive oil and heat up. While it's heating, take the ground cauliflower mix and create 8 patties that are 3 inches wide.

5. Fry them four at a time until browned on one side and then flip and cook the other side. Once they are done, transfer them to a plate.

6. For the tahini sauce, simply combine all the ingredients in a blender and blend them until they are smooth.

7. Serve the dish with tahini sauce.

Asparagus Quiche

When it is time to make some quick quiches, then nothing comes close to this receipt. The parmesan and mozzarella just compliment the spinach and asparagus that goes into the dish.

Ingredients

- 8 ounces asparagus (cooked)
  - 6 eggs (beaten)
  - 2-½ cup mozzarella cheese (grated)
  - 2 cups baby spinach leaves
  - 2 tablespoons parmesan cheese (grated)
  - 2 cloves garlic (minced)
  - ½ teaspoon salt
  - ½ teaspoon pepper

Directions

1. Preheat the oven to about 375°F.
2. Take out a pie pan and lightly grease it with cooking spray.
3. Combine eggs with 2 cups of grated mozzarella cheese and garlic in a bowl. Mix them all together well.

4. Take out about ¼ of the egg mixture and set it aside for now.
5. In the remaining egg mixture, stir spinach leaves and pour into the prepared pan. Layer asparagus on top of egg mixture in pan.
6. Take out the ¼ egg mixture that you had set aside and then pour the mixture on top of the asparagus.
7. Add remaining mozzarella and all the parmesan cheese on top.
8. Pop the pie pan into the oven and bake for about 30 minutes or until you notice the edges start to turn brown.

Mediterranean Pasta

The Mediterranean conjures up images of the sun, beaches, and clear waters. Get ready to bring those images to life with this pasta recipe.

Ingredients

- 10 kalamata olives (halved)
  - 5 cloves garlic (minced)
  - 2 large zucchinis (cut using spiralizer)
  - 2 tablespoons olive oil
  - 2 tablespoons capers
  - 2 tablespoons parsley (chopped)
  - 2 tablespoons butter
  - 1 cup spinach (packed)
  - ½ teaspoon salt
  - ½ teaspoon pepper
  - ¼ cup sun-dried tomatoes
  - ¼ cup parmesan cheese (shredded)
  - ¼ cup feta cheese (crumbled)

Directions

1. Take out a large pan and place it over medium heat. Add zucchini, spinach, olive oil, butter, garlic, salt, and pepper. Sauté

until zucchini is tender and spinach is wilted. Drain excess liquid.

2. To the pan, add sun-dried tomatoes, capers, parsley, and kalamata olives. Mix in and sauté for 2-3 minutes.

3. Remove from heat and toss all the ingredients with parmesan and feta cheeses before serving.

Cheesy Risotto

This risotto oozes with all the cheesy goodness. What makes it standout is the added flavor of Dijon mustard that brings out the flavors of all the ingredients in the dish.

Ingredients

- 3 tablespoons freshly chopped chives
  - 1 medium cauliflower
  - 1 small white onion (chopped)
  - 1 cup vegetable stock
  - 1 teaspoon Dijon mustard
  - 1 cup cheddar cheese (shredded)
  - 1 cup parmesan cheese (grated)
  - ½ teaspoon salt
  - ½ teaspoon pepper
  - ¼ cup ghee

Directions

1. We are going to make the cauliflower rice first. If the cauliflower has leaves, then remove them first and put them in a food processor. You are not going to make a smooth paste out of it. Rather, you are going to process the cauliflower into tiny bits.

2. Once you have done that, take out a large pan and place it over medium heat. Grease the pan with ghee or butter. Once hot,

add the finely chopped onion and cook until lightly browned.

3. Add in the cauliflower rice and mix all the ingredients well.

4. Cook for just a few minutes and pour in the vegetable stock. Cook for another 5 minutes or until the cauli-rice is tender. Meanwhile, grate the cheddar and parmesan cheese.

5. Add the mustard into the pan, stir the ingredients, and take off the heat.

6. Add the grated cheese and mix well. Keep some parmesan cheese for garnish. Add the freshly chopped chives and also keep some for garnish. Add the salt and pepper.

7. Finally, place the risotto into serving bowls and top with the remaining parmesan cheese and chives.

Chapter 6: Tasteful Snacks and Desserts

It is time to hit the sweet spot! What better way to do it than by indulging in some sweet goodness and lip smacking snacks that will make you wonder, "Why didn't I try this before?"

Cauliflower with Tzatziki Dip

Enjoy cauliflowers? Then why not compliment them with a dip?

Ingredients

- 2 cups cauliflower florets
  - 2 tablespoons chives (chopped)
  - 1 cup sour cream
  - 1 tablespoon ranch seasoning
  - 1 cucumber (diced)
  - ½ package cream cheese

Directions

1. Take out the electric mixer.
2. Add the cream cheese into it and beat it until it looks smooth and creamy. You can also beat it manually if you like.
3. Add in the ranch seasoning and sour cream, then continue beating it for a couple of minutes.
4. Add in the chives and cucumbers. Place it in the refrigerator for at least half an hour before serving.

Macadamia Nuts Roasted in Curry

Enjoy curry so much that you are wondering if you can make something quickly without having to resort to a complex dish? You wish has been granted. This crunchy dish can be eaten with any lunch or dinner recipe.

Ingredients

- 2 cups macadamia nuts (preferably raw)
  - 1-½ tablespoons olive oil
  - 1 tablespoon curry powder
  - ½ teaspoon salt

Directions

1. Preheat the oven to 300°F. Take out a baking tray and line it with parchment.
2. Whisk together the olive oil, curry powder, and salt in a mixing bowl.
3. Toss in the macadamia nuts to coat, then spread it on the baking sheet.
4. Bake for 25 minutes until toasted, then cool to room temperature.

Chia and Coconut Pudding

The best part of the pudding is that you can enjoy them anytime. This pudding can be placed in the refrigerator and you can have it whenever you feel like enjoying a delightful snack.

Ingredients

- 2-¼ cup canned coconut milk
  - 1 teaspoon vanilla extract
  - 1 teaspoon liquid stevia

- ½ teaspoon salt
- ½ cup chia seeds

Directions

1. Take out a bowl and combine the coconut milk, vanilla, and salt.
2. Stir well and sweeten with stevia.
3. Whisk in the chia seeds and chill overnight.
4. Spoon into bowls and serve with chopped nuts or fruit.

Almond Butter Brownies with Chocolate

Who doesn't like brownies with chocolate? In these brownies, you are letting the bitterness of chocolate compliment the smoothness of the butter and the crunchiness of the almonds.

Ingredients

- 2 large eggs
  - 1 cup almond flour
  - 1 cup coconut oil
  - 1-½ teaspoons liquid stevia
  - ¾ cup unsweetened cocoa powder
  - ½ cup shredded unsweetened coconut
  - ½ teaspoon baking soda
  - ½ cup canned coconut milk
  - ¼ cup almond butter

Directions

1. Preheat the oven to 350°F. Take out a baking pan or tray and line it with aluminum foil.
2. Whisk together the almond flour, cocoa powder, coconut, and

baking soda in a mixing bowl.

3. In another bowl, beat together the coconut oil, coconut milk, eggs, and liquid stevia.
4. Stir the wet ingredients into the dry until just combined, then spread in the pan.
5. Melt the almond butter in the microwave until creamy.
6. Drizzle over the chocolate batter, then swirl gently with a knife.
7. Bake for 25 to 30 minutes until the center is set then cool completely, then cut into 16 equal pieces.

Cinnamon Bread

There is something about having a sweet and spicy combination of cinnamon bread. You can actually combine the bread with the brownie recipe that we just saw.

Ingredients

- 6 tablespoons canned coconut milk
  - 3 tablespoons melted coconut oil
  - 3 large eggs (whisked)
  - 2 tablespoons water
  - 1-¼ teaspoon ground cinnamon
  - 1 teaspoon baking soda
  - 1 teaspoon apple cider vinegar
  - 1 teaspoon liquid stevia
  - ½ cup coconut flour
  - ½ teaspoon salt
  - ¼ teaspoon baking powder

Directions

1. Preheat the oven to 350°F. Take out a loaf pan and grease it lightly with cooking spray.

2. Combine the coconut flour, cinnamon, baking soda, baking powder, and salt in a mixing bowl and stir well.
3. In another bowl, whisk together the coconut milk, oil, water, vinegar, and eggs.
4. Stir the wet ingredients into the dry, then sweeten to taste with stevia.
5. Spread the batter in the pan and cook for 25 to 30 minutes, then let cool.

Lemon Meringue Cookies

A little sweetness and plenty of lemon zest-ness to make this cookie a fan favorite.

Ingredients

- 2 cups cauliflower florets
  - 2 tablespoons chives (chopped)
  - 1 cup sour cream
  - 1 tablespoon ranch seasoning
  - 1 cucumber (diced)
  - ½ package cream cheese

Directions

1. Preheat the oven to 225°F. Take out a baking tray and line it with parchment.
2. Beat the egg whites in a bowl until soft peaks form.
3. Add the salt and stevia, then beat until stiff peaks form.
4. Fold in the lemon extract. Take out a piping bag and place all the ingredients into it.
5. Pipe the mixture onto the baking sheet in small rounds.
6. Bake for 50 to 60 minutes until dry.
7. Once done, take out the baking tray and allow it to cool before

serving.

Coconut Macaroons

I like to think of macaroons as delightful little cookies. But how can you make one that stays true to the macaroon spirit and still manages to be unique? You do this by this recipe.

Ingredients

- 3 large egg whites
  - 2 tablespoons powdered erythritol
  - 1 tablespoon coconut oil
  - 1 teaspoon vanilla extract
  - ½ cup unsweetened shredded coconut
  - ½ teaspoon coconut extract
  - ¼ cup almond flour

Directions

1. Preheat the oven to 400°F. Take out a baking tray and line it with parchment.
2. Combine the almond flour, coconut, and erythritol in a bowl. Mix them well.
3. In a separate bowl, add the coconut oil, then whisk in the extracts (vanilla and coconut).
4. Stir the mixtures from the first and second bowl together
5. Beat the egg whites in a bowl until stiff peaks form, then fold into the batter.
6. Spoon onto the baking sheet in even-sized mounds.
7. Bake for 7-9 minutes until the macaroons are just browned on the edges.

Vanilla Ice Cream with Coconut

This comfort food comes with the delightful flavor of coconut. And if you are wondering if it's difficult to make? Then worry not.

Ingredients

- 2 cups canned coconut milk (divided)
  - 1 tablespoon coconut oil
  - 1 teaspoon vanilla extract
  - ½ teaspoon liquid stevia

Directions

1. Take out a saucepan and place it over medium heat. Add the coconut oil in it. Then whisk in half of the coconut milk.
2. Bring to a boil, then reduce heat and simmer for 30 minutes.
3. Pour into a bowl and sweeten with stevia, then let cool to room temperature.
4. Stir in the vanilla extract, then pour the remaining coconut milk into a bowl.
5. Beat the coconut milk until stiff peaks form, then fold into the other mixture.
6. Spoon into a loaf pan and freeze until firm.

Ginger Cookies

Why add ginger as a small part of the meal when it can be the main component of it? Presenting, the ginger cookies!

Ingredients

- 1 cup coconut butter
  - 1 large egg
  - 1 teaspoon vanilla extract

- ½ cup powdered erythritol
- ½ teaspoon ground ginger
- ½ teaspoon baking soda
- ¼ teaspoon ground nutmeg
- ¼ teaspoon salt

Directions

1. Preheat the oven to 350°F. Take out a baking tray and line lit with parchment.
2. Place the coconut butter in a food processor with the egg and vanilla.
3. Blend until it becomes smooth then add the erythritol, ginger, baking soda, nutmeg, and salt.
4. Pulse until it forms a dough, then shape into 16 small balls.
5. Place the balls on the baking sheet and flatten slightly.
6. Bake for 12-15 minutes until the edges are browned then cool.

Chapter 7: The 28-Day Meal Plan

So many delicious recipes to choose from, but how can one plan out their meals in such a way that they can enjoy all the dishes while at the same time, spread them out really well over the course of a week.

Well, thankfully, you have this 28-day meal plan to help you out. Yes, ice creams are included too. And the chai. And the cookies. And the, well, you get the point.

Week 1

Day	Breakfast	Lunch	Snack	Dinner
1	Soft Keto Cream Cheese Pancakes	Vegetarian Taco Salad with Avocado Lime Dressing	Macadamia Nuts Roasted in Curry	Baked Mushrooms, Italian Style
2	Almond Muffins with Butter	Egg Salad On Lettuce	Chia and Coconut Pudding	Spinach Ricotta Bake
3	Classic Omelet, Keto Style!	Spring Salad Topped with Shaved Parmesan	Almond Butter Brownies with Chocolate	White Egg Pizza
4	Protein Pancakes with a Cinnamon Twist	Spinach and Avocado Salad with Almonds	Cinnamon Bread	Roasted Mushrooms with Feta, Herbs, and Red Pepper
5	Crispy Chai Waffles	Quick Chopped Salad (When You Cannot Wait)	Lemon Meringue Cookies	Eggplant Hash, The Moroccon Way
6	Egg Muffins with Tomato and Mozzarella	Avocado, Lettuce, and Tomato Sandwich	Coconut Macaroons	Asparagus Quiche
7	Scrambled Eggs with Spinach and Parmesan	Artichoke and Spinach Casserole	Vanilla Ice Cream with Coconut	Mediterranean Pasta

Week 2

Day	Breakfast	Lunch	Snack	Dinner
8	Cinnamon Waffles	Shaking Shakshuka!	Ginger Cookies	Falafel with Tahini Sauce
9	Pumpin' Pumpkin Spice Waffles	Cheese and Broccoli Fritters	French Ice Cream	Cheesy Risotto
10	Keto Oatmeal Cinnamon Spiced	Stuffed Zucchini with Marinara	Almond Butter Brownies with Chocolate	Spinach Ricotta Bake
11	Keto Mexican Breakfast Fiesta!	Cauliflower Steak Take	Cinnamon Bread	White Egg Pizza
12	Shufflin' Breakfast Souffle	Limey Creamy Coleslaw	Macadamia Nuts Roasted in Curry	Roasted Mushrooms with Feta, Herbs, and Red Pepper
13	Cauliflower Hash Browns	The Greek Wrapper	Chia and Coconut Pudding	Eggplant Hash, The Moroccon Way
14	Soft Keto Cream Cheese Pancakes	Egg Drop and Zucchini Soup	Lemon Meringue Cookies	Baked Mushrooms, Italian Style

Week 3

Day	Breakfast	Lunch	Snack	Dinner
15	Scrambled Eggs with Spinach and Parmesan	Avocado, Lettuce, and Tomato Sandwich	Coconut Macaroons	Falafel with Tahini Sauce
16	Egg Muffins with Tomato and Mozzarella	Artichoke and Spinach Casserole	Vanilla Ice Cream with Coconut	Cheesy Risotto
17	Crispy Chai Waffles	Spinach and Avocado Salad with Almonds	Cinnamon Bread	Spinach Ricotta Bake
18	Protein Pancakes with a Cinnamon Twist	Quick Chopped Salad (When You Cannot Wait)	Macadamia Nuts Roasted in Curry	Baked Mushrooms, Italian Style
19	Classic Omelet, Keto Style!	Egg Salad On Lettuce	Chia and Coconut Pudding	Spinach Ricotta Bake
20	Almond Muffins with Butter	Spring Salad Topped with Shaved Parmesan	Almond Butter Brownies with Chocolate	White Egg Pizza
21	Pumpin' Pumpkin Spice Waffles	Vegetarian Taco Salad with Avocado Lime Dressing	Cinnamon Bread	Roasted Mushrooms with Feta, Herbs, and Red Pepper

Week 4

Day	Breakfast	Lunch	Snack	Dinner
22	Soft Keto Cream Cheese Pancakes	The Greek Wrapper	Almond Butter Brownies with Chocolate	White Egg Pizza
23	Cauliflower Hash Browns	Egg Drop and Zucchini Soup	Cinnamon Bread	Roasted Mushrooms with Feta, Herbs, and Red Pepper
24	Shufflin' Breakfast Souffle	Cauliflower Steak Take	Macadamia Nuts Roasted in Curry	Eggplant Hash, The Moroccon Way
25	Keto Mexican Breakfast Fiesta!	Limey Creamy Coleslaw	Ginger Cookies	Baked Mushrooms, Italian Style
26	Keto Oatmeal Cinnamon Spiced	Cheese and Broccoli Fritters	French Ice Cream	Spinach Ricotta Bake
27	Crispy Chai Waffles	Stuffed Zucchini with Marinara	Almond Butter Brownies with Chocolate	Falafel with Tahini Sauce
28	Egg Muffins with Tomato and Mozzarella	Shaking Shakshuka!	Coconut Macaroons	Cheesy Risotto

NOTE: You can have a cup of black coffee without any sugar in the morning if you like. Here are other drinks that you can have with your breakfast:

- Keto Spice Latte Boost
- Smooth Avocado and Kale Smoothie
- Almond Butter Protein Smoothie

- Blueberry and Beets Smoothie
- Green Smoothie for Detoxifying
- Protein Smoothie with Creamy Chocolate
- Keto Tea

You can also have the following with your lunch or dinner:

- Egg Soup
- Spinach Cauliflower Soup

The following dips or sauces can also be used to compliment any dish:

- Cauliflower Hummus
- Veggie Red Curry
- Cauliflower with Tzatziki Dip

Conclusion

Finally, we are at the end of our journey.

But that does not mean your personal journey has ended.

The hardest part about keto is not starting it, but maintaining it. This is why you should never give into peer pressure. Do not easily be tempted by sugar-rich and carb-rich foods. Stay true to your journey because at the end of it, you will gain incredible benefits.

Most importantly, do not forget to exercise.

That's right! Just because you are on a keto diet does not mean that you can to skip your workout routines.

When you are heading into a better lifestyle, you are not only focusing on what you eat, but how well you take care of your body as well.

Getting regular exercise is important. Not staying in one position for too long is also important.

With that, I wish you good look on the road to a healthier tomorrow. Stay healthy!

Lightning Source UK Ltd.
Milton Keynes UK
UKHW042327040522
402515UK00003B/48